The Sky Was Once a Dark Blanket

The National Poetry Series was established in 1978 to ensure the publication of five collections of poetry annually through five participating publishers. The Series has been funded over the years by Amazon Literary Partnership, the Gettinger Family Foundation, Bruce Gibney, HarperCollins Publishers, The Stephen and Tabitha King Foundation, Lannan Foundation, Newman's Own Foundation, Anna and Olafur Olafsson, Penguin Random House, the Poetry Foundation, Hawthornden Foundation, Elise and Steven Trulaske, and the National Poetry Series Board of Directors.

THE NATIONAL POETRY SERIES WINNERS
OF THE 2023 OPEN COMPETITION

Field Guide for Accidents by Albert Abonado
Chosen by Mahogany L. Browne for Beacon Press

Post-Volcanic Folk Tales by Mackenzie Schubert Poloyni Donnelly
Chosen by Ishion Hutchinson for Akashic Books

The Sky Was Once A Dark Blanket by Kinsale Drake
Chosen by Jacqueline Trimble for University of Georgia Press

Playing With The Jew by Ava Winter
Chosen by Sean Hill for Milkweed Editions

the space between men by Mia S. Willis
Chosen by Morgan Parker for Penguin

The Sky Was Once a Dark Blanket

POEMS

Kinsale Drake

SELECTED BY JACQUELINE ALLEN TRIMBLE

The University of Georgia Press   *Athens*

Published by the University of Georgia Press
Athens, Georgia 30602
www.ugapress.org
© 2024 by Kinsale Drake
All rights reserved
Designed by Erin Kirk
Set in Garamond Premier Pro

Most University of Georgia Press titles are
available from popular e-book vendors.

Printed digitally

Library of Congress Cataloging-in-Publication Data

Names: Drake, Kinsale, author. | Trimble, Jacqueline Allen, compiler.
Title: The sky was once a dark blanket : poems / Kinsale Drake ;
    selected by Jacqueline Allen Trimble.
Description: Athens : The University of Georgia Press, 2024. |
    Series: The National Poetry Series
Identifiers: LCCN 2024014833 (print) | LCCN 2024014834
    (ebook) | ISBN 9780820367309 (paperback) | ISBN 9780820367316
    (epub) | ISBN 9780820367323 (pdf)
Subjects: LCGFT: Poetry.
Classification: LCC PS3604.R3525 S59 2024 (PRINT) | LCC PS3604.R3525
    (EBOOK) | DDC 811/.6—dc23/eng/20240417
LC record available at https://lccn.loc.gov/2024014833
LC ebook record available at https://lccn.loc.gov/2024014834

For my parents, my siblings, Masani, my cheii,

my great Uncle Buck and his songs, my great Aunt Mary

and her peaches, my home, and all of my family

that has poured their light into me.

Nizhoni, it is beautiful.

CONTENTS

The Sky Was Once a Dark Blanket

spangled

enough about you: airwaves
in bloom, mouthpiece

on fire. I must sing
the hum of the yucca

and icy heartbeat
of river. I must sing

our grandparents' blues
knocked down in the grasses

and thick in the farmhouse.
O, like Jimi's guitar I must sing—

dirty sing blister let the sound
rip the sky

rush of birds spooked
from deep in our throats—

our song:

*

I.

August

My mother's soft instrument, I am stomping
          at 11 a.m. on god's holiest day, my grandmother
turning up her hands in something like protest,
          her face just softened by the rainbow of a smile.
Oh joy, I overturn the sweet peas in the garden
          with my bare feet, instruments
                    of disaster, instruments
          of my mother, who used to sneak out to border towns
          and line dance with cowboys. We miss the days
          the rain fell on our foreheads and the kettle
          boiled over. When I want to call up
          the memory of these women, I sit
                    with the familiar orchestra
                    of scratched up CDs.
          Shhh! Just there—the instruments
of our own destruction and births. Umbilical cords.
          Planting season. I want
                    to roll in the mud and be a mother.
          I want the seeds to two-step on my skin.

FOR MILDRED BAILEY, *in three parts*

The voice   glides
from the turntable
        guiding him out of the kitchen, out
of the city to his father's front porch
        on the reservation   no mouthpiece
no anthropologist   no audience
        Except the trees   brick of earth
the clay   wide body receiving   soft
        sounds of birds   applause

It was spring   when he first
heard the sound of wings
            in the city
                    The door of a New York club
swung open   on E. 55th   Miss Mildred
and her wide voice   rivering   the smoke
Her lips   heartberry-
        red   in the lights

Lenapehoking

            heaving towards a sound

                        beneath the pavement

& Who Remembers Mildred Bailey?

She had a clear voice, light and steady. She loved Bessie Smith. She
had an Indian mother.

Glimmering with the three Rhythm Boys:

Seventeen, she was on her own.

I wanted to forget you

In L.A., Bing Crosby to the scene. Under the law, she's not a
human being.

Oh, Rocking Chair Lady. What land do you reach
when you sing of *home*?

Lover, come back

Her voice blue smoke,

Lover, come back to me

dead at 44.

The sky was blue and high above

In New York, all train tracks lead away from Georgia.

The moon was new and so was love

Xylophonist, warm instrument,

Everyone caught their breath and slept.

This eager heart of mine was singing

Crossing New York nightclubs until her death—

What color is the river?

It's so quiet in this lonely pantheon

Lover, where can you be?

Kitchen Table, or When Mildred Bailey Sings:

Gramophones were weapons, swallowing
the dying songs—
voices

are still muted
in the dust bowl
of those English libraries.

But her voice is clear
as the Chattahoochee,
wide and glittering,

breaching the shadows of the Blue Angel.
Oh, winged music,
red-tongued

notes on 55th where
red boys in strange cities once stopped dead
and dreamed of Georgia

again: instruments of their fathers,
forefathers, and further.
Her angel voice

brings them home
to Cherokee,
the whooping crane.

She lets her sons fumble back,
led by soft sonata
and the bird tracks.

Wax Cylinder

There was a voice calling in the night from the tin
behind the glass. The receptionist noted the sound

of cicadas circling near the women's bathroom. Cylinder,
cicada, legs moving round and round and a brass-
colored mouth.

Flat glass, laser-protected
            mahogany drawers. The custodian was scared

of Indian ghosts in the half-light,
            how the wax cylinders
looked like tree trunks. Every night
            the voice would not stop singing
as he defogged his windshield and zig-zagged home.

The voice trickled
            after him, out the front gate.
I can't say anything new
            about her—she knows herself and her path
home—her desert emerald, or the eye socket
            of a sow skull. There are only one hundred
reruns in the body, her body a weapon
            when it sings. To UNRAVEL, like the sun,
which spills itself along, I speak back
            to this voice.

I tell her a story.
Shimá, I call her.
I am a woman remembering her place
among the stars. The voice
will never be lost
while constellations
        pulse against the sheaths of glass.
Come home,
        scattering between us
in our language full of light.

You survive the end of the world in Kayenta, AZ with your mother

in the Blue Coffee Pot. The waitress sets two tall plastic Coke cups
of water before you both. Today, everyone must be especially generous.

All around: nalis with their tight *tsiiyéeł* and jewels and long velvet skirts
that brush the floor. Your mother says the turquoise

tear drops are a shield. Never take them off. The women smile
at their grandchildren. They don't sit with any husbands. You've become

attuned again to their little song. Your mother says to you that a plate
of mutton will cure any ailment. You both eat with your hands. You could

have cried. Later, it's back up to Monument Valley
where the rocks look like women, hushed together. KTNN buzzes:

I wanted to be your everything. The only station for miles. Rock formations
give nothing away. *Not everything,* you think. Your mother

tells you to use the grease left on your hands to heal your lips. You smear
your fingers across an eye instead. Then the other. The monuments flicker

and you hum a song about women with straight backs
and eyelashes pretty with rain, a song you heard most

while your grandmother still lived
and the roosters rampaged in her yard as she bent

over the fire with cardboard and a poker
and your mother smiled and swayed you on her hip,

looking off, off toward the mountain,
feeding you mutton with her hands.

NDN Heartbreak Song

After Joy Harjo

Albuquerque phonebooth:

   Next door a boy I loved
    who loved my cousin

It's only funny
   if you're not an **NDN**

   The desert
  teaches us
  not to give all
   of ourselves away

Wish I'd remembered
   burning piñon
    & clay deposits
     Before I dreamed
  cool rush of river
    that dries in August
  & frogs
   that disappear
     for eight months
  or more
   at a time

I have loved you,
      he had said,
           since before I have known you:
     letters gutted
        monarch wings
            on the highway
    as Albuquerque
      skated past

      & the phonebooths whipped by
      small blue spines

 & I

     Swept up
        from the line
           Lifted high by a gale,
               Brought too far
               from a shoulder of water

everything is weird in the NE because there are no NDN
memorials, only NDN names

The marsh islands with their little tufted backs
        Someone's home,
            everywhere is always someone's home
Late sun fills the window of the Amtrak N.E.
Mouths open in the trees, in the mud
When our bones are found
        it's called a haunting
            Where do the birds go? Who
gets a funeral? Everything is a burial
        ground, even the sky.
                In the old ways, this was someone's back,
The constellations bulletholes straight through
        his stomach
                Blasted with light—
        How many NDNs must die here
for anyone to know?
        The train babbles on about everything
else. I don't want
        to talk about the land so much—
I don't wanna eco-NDN,
        But the marsh grasses
            look like the most loved and lonely
            parts of my body
        Where do songs go when it is dark?
            What names
                moved through these trees,
            The soft now-grass
                The underbellies of the leaves

prickly pear woman blues

& the church is quiet
        in the plum dusk/
all my youth:
        sunsets tinged with want/

& the white couch
        from my childhood home/
that smelled of dryer sheets/
        wet stone

my smashed heat
        on the rug/
where my white bf
        shoved me from
                the scarlet/

my hot pink heart/
        the horses all gone home/
sagebrush rubbing/
        dogs chained
                in the yards/

they arc their spines
for sweetness

leave the hot wound/ scarlet
        never/ just a bruise

Remembering

"Dreams are poems your body writes." –Sandra Cisneros

How do I start a story I never lived?

I think I remember stories because they are violent.

Or because there is music.

My mother had a horse.

Her father held the horse's face gently.

I make this up,   because I know he was gentle.

I know he listened to his radio on the way to work.

The snow in the North where my mother went to school,

I have never seen it fall.

Nor lived in 1983.

Recently, she told us how the men there

Ate at everything with their fingers.

My body dreams less tragic NDN things.

She stitches compositions,

When she can.

But at the very least,

My body dreams.

II.

Alabama, 1992

My father grieves his reflection
in the sopping nightheat

of cricket-song. My sister watches
with strange eyes

from a crib in the corner.
My mother finishes a puzzle

with her quiet heart—belly
big, the moon

of her luminous
in the gas lamps.

Her father passed
the year before

and she will soon give birth
to a child who will grow

to restore antiques
and hate every mirror

they find their fathers in.
And in Utah, somewhere

my grandmother is turning
Hank Williams off

on their family radio
as the yeast bread rises

on the oven and the garden
twists outside around itself.

She will not listen to him
again for many, many years,

each of her children scattered
like Coyote's many stars.

Sound of under-water

1. In winter we are closest to the ocean that once held nautiloids, corals, cartilaginous fishes. Diné tour guides make signs on the side of the road, usher cars into invisible parking spots amid pools of half-melted snow. Guides remove nothing, pushing bills into their pockets.

2. Clouds leave our bodies like great whales when the desert swims in song from a truck's thrown-open door. The heat escapes into the ocean of sky.

3. White historians claim that the Spanish brought over the first horses. Modern genetics and scientific opinion suggest that these animals are the same ancestors that once roamed the continent before traveling to Eurasia. The ocean had given way by this time to swamp, ice, and fire. Rocks are the oldest storytellers, my friend Gusti tells me. The Badlands shrink behind us, gray teeth swimming in ghosts.

4. It was a warm, shallow sea. This brings comfort during a blizzard in the Northeast.

5. Mid-19th century scientists claimed to know these fossils better by cataloging, sectioning off, drilling holes, carting off to museums. Locals told stories. Here is one:

6. Glaciers recede from the Southwest, and the basin dries up. Much later, farmers try to bottle every last teardrop.

7. A whale's song can be heard from 10,000 miles away.

8. Today, the formations of Capitol Reef mushroom towards the sky. In the 40s, the rocks were white with fire.

9. We loop, loop, loop *the Badlands*. Mako sica. Is it all the same ocean? From here to *Canyon De Chelly*. Tsegi. I say it is, out loud, so the tourists lose their footing. I roll down my window, a new friend for these northern fossils.

10. At night, the rocks glow. Uranium, yellow pollen, bone dust. All the once-children of the ocean orbit the seascape.

Coming-of-age song

Yucca song: what season do you come in?
      Girls, with your soft furrows,
hands thick with sun. We are so scared of knowing
that which dies too soon. All around us,
      the hills open. Their seasons abalone,
dark jet, turquoise, white shell blinding
in the dusk-light. The song is sticky
          like a child's fingers. Girls, I wish
we had been gentler
      with ourselves. Juniper boughs snap
against calves and there is no good
      way back. This is a good thing,
we are told, as the ground swallows
      us up to our arms. Girls, we are lost
in corn meal the same heat
      as our bodies.
This is a good thing. Hold
      your breath.
Bake your blind cake.
      Count. This is
        a good thing.

Your Return

Last night we fought
again in my dreams.
It's funny how
when we do this,
our small step-dance,
you only speak
in Navajo and I
understand. This time,
it was the egg-blue
kettle or tóshchíín pot
left on the stove
too long, bottom
roasted black. Or
my favorite dog
you'd kicked at
a bit too hard,
like the time you swung
to save the last chicken
and your water
broke and my father
cried out from
the window. You
never said I love
you after we fought
like this. But in
my dreams, we
cry at the table
afterwards,

and it is almost
like surfacing
together
I wake up
gasping

thinking
the sound
of the kitchen
door opening
is you,
running
from the table
to the dog
closing its heavy jaws
on the rooster,
yelling
hágo, shhh!
come here,
come here.

after Sacred Water (Our Emergence)

I.

in the summers we would flock to my great-aunt's
swimming hole   down the canyon
dizzy from the jumbling in a truck bed
poke at the tadpoles squirming in the red clay
my mother watched from orchard shade
she had been down here many years before
with her sisters   her brothers
picking apples, following the bend
of the river   leading the goats to the wayside to drink
now the water glooms
with cow manure   uranium
we trace the mud with our eyes
watch the petroglyphs stretch
in the shadows
miss the feeling of the sun   wicking river from our skin

II.

in 1956/ the glen canyon dam began construction/ with an explosion/
was hit with a demolition blast keyed/ by the push of a button/
in the oval office/ the bottom of the canyon/ dotted by navajo/
ute/ paiute footprints/
still cooling/ the explosion/ a scar in the earth still aching
with uranium mines/ yellowcake/ yellow corn/ tumbled
in the runoff/ what do you call ancestral homestead/stopped
like a kitchen sink/ the water/ of your people
redirected to ranches/ fatten cattle that render the san juan undrinkable/
quench the white men/ in bars/ that don't admit NDNs/ water
and mineral/ packed into bombshells/ how do you drown
by your own artery/ today
the lake has never been shallower/ a drought
of its own becoming/ not even time to weep/ before the crossing
before the fleeing/ marina of familiar fossils/ zebra mussels
scour the bones of old adobe/ still
beneath the surface/ the ancient sun rendered closer
every day/ as the ranchers lament the withering/ the tourists
dock their houseboats/ the people who have known
this land/ see the slickrock
still/ emerging

III.

in the third world, coyote took the water monster's baby
so the water monster decided to make it rain endlessly
the water rose and choked the peaks
of sacred mountains

the beings that lived there
did not know where to escape the flood
& what saved the world was a reed curling
into the sky   a way to climb out   into a fourth world

IV.

There are things that remain stolen   that holy people
weep for   And others look to us with upturned hands
          Ask where the reeds come from
                Flee to the highest peaks
                                Dream of another world
                                They can scurry into
                Through a wound in the sky   They created

We have no answer for them
          We have known this the entire time
So we tell our stories   Go to the water
          Tend this land
                & remember

Theme for the nautical cowboy

My mother wouldn't let me go to the rodeo
        when I was younger, so I jet off with my girl
in her truck to a George Strait song. It's in our cosmology
        to chase the tails of dogs over the horizon.
The sky stretches, map of strange stars.
        I list the star signs of my exes, none of them
from Texas. We cheers our Baja Blasts.
        Almost all sacred things are blue. *Baby blue,*
Baby blue. You joke that you'll never date a white boy,
        eh, you sing a love song to shit-straight hair and nighttime
eyes. The compass needle stays glued to the moon.
        I catch your eyes in every mirror.
There was once a prehistoric ocean all around us,
        even whales. We puff out
the great swimming shapes
        of their bodies.
This layer of rock, trilobites.
        This layer, some ancient eel. How small we are,
how funny. Massive fish-ghosts
        vibrate to George Strait. Time is read backwards
in the rock-body: oldest to the top, magma pushing
        what's fresh to the surface. Your hand
skims the deep blue
        sandstone, these long-cooled shells.
Tear drop, turquoise sliver of horizon, the creeping river
        invisible in the dark. *Here's to you,*
here's to you, ancient and alive.
The sky stretches, full of old and older ghosts,
        our once and forever wading pool.

Navajo-English Dictionary

Faded text   crushed bugs in the sand
    Small dots   where ink has skipped
The page   didzétsoh – peaches
Didzédík'ózhii – choke berry
Didzé – berry   berries   I am so starved

    for words   creamy pinks   sparrows

shirt tails   blood clots   quails—
    eyes
        river
    the page   /we will look at it/

/we sit/   diniibiih, dah   the words grow—

    jet-black   shell-white

in my throat – diildooh

    it is about   to burst

words climb   spring stalks   slow

unlike when I was a girl   memorizing books
    in English   diitaa'—they/ it—
        fell apart—
went to pieces
    shattered

Noise beginning   at the tip of

    The entrance   /we sit/

Corral the pages inside   every half-rainbowed

      Consonant,   spine

rising up the page   like song   smoke

corn

        it is rising

      dilchxoshí – it is about

           to   dilchxoshí

      it is about   to

Put on that KTNN

My mother was raised on Patsy Cline
and Hank Williams country
that bounced in on her father's radio.

Even today, I know I am nearing home
when the pop music crackles
into KTNN, licks

of fluent Navajo flitting between
Loretta Lynn and Johnny Cash.
They are interludes, too,

for drumbeats and throaty covers
of well-loved tunes put on
by some local boys' gas station

banjo and hot-rocket guitar,
a strong woman that sings
the seasons over a hand drum.

Then it is back
to more Loretta Lynn.
All contradictions

find a home in the body, the insect-skin
of the car sluicing the Arizona desert
as the cicadas pick up their grand

instruments. How else to know
you enter a land of monuments, not
a wasteland, loved by radio waves

and peach trees
and silly dogs that bridge
the distance between a chapter house

and the nearest Sonics in a city.
The moon rocks darken into pine,
pine into slickrock,

and the whole world remembers
what it once was—
grand ocean: sun, plankton, pearl,

blood, ancestor, cloud. Radio rainbows
the most violent parts of the land
thrashed by thunderstorms and sea

as the rattles pick up their backing track
and Hank Williams rolls in
all over again, easy and easy

and blue.

III.

Kylie Jenner Collage of the American West

Hear her Martian war whoop
in her Monument Valley Mars

Clouds? They are planets in the blue,
left long ago by red men

who talked strange and fell
to earth. (They are not naturally-
occurring, according
to her science.)

She builds resorts
from the waterways,
space stations in the stone,

Vacuums through a happy road
& cuts us out

Pastes us back in a corner of the sky

The space we leave
              Our erratic burial
She's collaged this:

Our absence ephemera of a future saran-wrapped
and refrigerated,
Her mystic desert palace

powered by nuclear swimming pools,
& totem poles that drink the rivers

We mourn from our distant space-rock

She leads the influencers
in eulogy
over crystal goblets filled
with oil:
> *The red men just didn't know*
> *what they had!*

THE GREENHOUSE

After Tayi Tibble

I want to weave this correctly.   I hung around the orchids, the
insectivores,
          and cacti. This was my first winter, when the world   grew
stiff and brilliant-
white. Nothing was familiar   except the desert rooms, so I'd stalk
the rows
          of spiny Latin names between my classes until my sweater-
neck
collected sweat.   Prickly pear, the great saguaro   I missed
the chollas most
          of all. I want to weave this in   correctly. I want to weave
them space

to breathe. My cousin collected prickly pear   in dirty Tupperware
one summer
          and I was almost afraid to touch them   small pink bodies
bleeding over the skin   of plastic   and here I was
ashamed   tracing columns of subjects so easily uprooted
          their small stakes   denoting translations   places
of origin   I want
          to weave this in correctly: My grandmother's house
nestled in desert shade, but here
          they were: agave   piñon   two thousand miles
from where she lived
          I was swimming   beneath the heat lamps
in a year that nearly   brought the roof down
          with snow

41

In the National Museum of the American Indian

you are
cruising through a gallery
    gazing at Suzan and Russell and Hank,
    photos of **AIM** with

long hair
parted down the middle, beads
    bright at the throats of frozen protestors
    when, so suddenly

you think
of your father, his hardened
    hands and voice that would shake itself violent,
    but how once when you

were small,
you came to **NMAI**,
    and surrounded by white people, he shook
    his long hair out from

its tie,
stopped in front of each photo,
    and you saw his eyes grow soft as they some-
    times would, deep in the

summers
when your mother brought čhaŋpȟá
    and kissed him gently. It was quiet, then,
    when the wild rice bloomed,

when he
did not hide himself from you.

Creation Story Blues

An Urban Indian belongs to the city, and cities belong to the earth.
—Tommy Orange

This is a desert like any other: towers
like cacti suck water from the sky.
Aloes shadow the cold-dark
if the Santa Anas blow in early.

Rivers are scarce. The A Line,
thin blue vein, spits us out
at Long Beach, so we drive
everywhere instead. I ask you

questions from the passenger side
because I love to watch you stitch the world
together. *It's all the same,* you say.
This place is a burial ground. Ash curls

across the 101 as fire claims
a row of palms. You remind me
that this city is homeland, too,
though it burns more often.

So we speak kindly to the land
when we can. Recognize the Hills
sloping like arroyo banks, the winding
highways carved like canyons.

*The sky was once a dark
blanket.* Your lips point to the lights
shivering downtown. Almost stars,
they spiral, startlingly bright

through the windshield. *Coyote threw*
up a basket of stars to shatter the black
into brilliance. Tonight, the cars
are white-fast comets slicing back

and forth across this concrete body.
Do the ghosts, too, feel comforted
in the haze as you sing me
the birth of the Milky Way?

The year the An*sazi Inn burned down

Because in a room with popcorn ceilings my grandmother
lay dying. Because that was about the time I wore out
The Black Parade on scratched CD. Because I was too young
to know the beetle-skin of grief. Bad excuse. I knew ghosts
that skimmed the desert-rim: earth-surface graves, shells
of prairie dogs and eagles on the highway, in the heat.

Because if you're shit-scared enough or brown
enough, everything can be an omen. Because to get over
the mountains, my grandfather never stopped running.
The anxiety that precedes certain death. Maybe it buzzed
in the A/C, familiar-sweet and river-cold. Through our veins,
it begged for just a light. Once-flickered gaze. Then, a flame.

Eulogy for the Cantina on Chapel St. that's transformed
into another bank

I feel god in this Taco Bell tonight:
Cheese, beans, rice, the witching hour

of missing someone. My mother
liked to cook with the worst kind of flour.

My father snuck sips of sweating drinks
clutched in my sister's little fingers. This

is the spot to lean into a table of alma mater
jackets and bask in the humidity

of frying dough. We are all here
for the same reasons, aching toward

what we desire most: a drunken gaze,
shaking the winter from our hair,

remembering a mother's taco shells
and refusing to wipe away the grease.

Navajo Mountain

My grandpa's house collapsed. I was looking out
The window, to a photograph of a daughter
Gone far away. Filled with thorns. I made love once
On that bed. Unfortunately, I told the boy I loved him
Where the electrical wiring and the insulation
Now weave a rug beneath the yawning roof.
My mother sends a text message, a photo of the bright
Pink. My insides. When I was little, I swallowed my grandma's
Iron pills and shit stuff black. The night. The inside
Of a lover's eye. Let's be fancy
About it, please. On the way
To the doctor's, my mother fed me orange chips,
Green soda, blue bubblegum, pink candy. I dreamed
Of my warm bed at home, my grandpa and his sweet tooth,
His bum stuck out playing basketball. My mother
Let me piss like a racehorse, and I laughed
For days. I let it almost kill me, the way that roof
Laughed inwards and heaved open. All the fallout.
Honey, can you remember what color
The insides were? In the photo, the couple is looking
Out towards the light. Their daughter is somewhere
There, babbling. She has not had her heart
Stop yet. From a man. There she goes,
With her shiny chrome
Heart. Inheritance. Stupid
As a songbird, but singing nonetheless.

You rock with the rose quartz, the sweetgrass, the cedar. In the
summer, our city smells almost like dusk on the rez. The reservoirs
too shallow, we imagine an ocean, the one that covered the Four
Corners. The Citibank building. Hook a right down Bunker Hill,
the one with the city Indians. Their ghosts shadow the eucalyptus
trees. Let them haunt you. I like it

that way: Up the 101, thick scarlet vein. I let you go bumper to
bumper, reclaim the land between each car. *Fuck it,* you honk, *Let's
be sovereign!* We riot in the fumes. Smoke lavender, tobacco, weeds.
Logically, the land's been dead a long time. The smog says otherwise,

the way it rises out of the Valley every other week. A long breath let
go. The Santa Anas carry the scents back to us that they tried to get
rid of. Inhale. A long line of trucks breaks

the jagged edges. We stop the car, hot, off Crenshaw.
When you hop out, you swear the ground kicks
just a little bit again beneath your feet.

IV.

(Re)location

Salt Lake City boasts white tabernacles,
half-filled parks, a mineral
highway, and archives so vast
they fill mountainsides.
One summer, we researched our family
genealogy there, surrounded by giddy Mormons.
Their screens flickered with famous
relatives: a Custer, Jackson, Theodore,
Kit. Nothing came up on ours,
so we went and got burgers at a place
that sold no liquor. The burgers
were okay. But we shared our shakes
and secret smiles and imagined
ourselves renegades in that room.
Old-West-portrait: an Indian girl
on the run with no records and no documents,
her windburned father clutching
his sarsaparilla. We had infiltrated
the saloon and city hall.
I locked eyes in the burger joint
with the confidence of a pistol-whipper.
The room stirred.
It smelled of grass
and gunsmoke.
I would not be moved again.

Notebook

I have taken to cataloging the kindnesses
        that surprise me: When the frogs returned,
small and wriggling across the sand
        with a vengeance. My meds, kicking in
on Los Flores street, where months ago I rear-ended
        the smog
of an ex. The thin blanket of rain that fell
        and our spooked, hurried steps
as we outran the dark. *Rumours'* record sleeve
propped up like an altar
        by my sister,
two months after my first heartbreak.
Joy will come,
        like the frogs,
                more often. Maze its way
through the understep
        of heavy boots. Let the song play,
again and again. May the needle
        wheel & wheel & wheel

Hollywood Indian

for Layli Long Soldier

I lay me down
across the metro tracks

Bless the parking lot where
I kissed a city NDN

There are lullabies downtown:
the desert moans at night

bringing the smell of cold
or a bloody nose

White hippies smoke, waist-deep
in overwatered native gardens

We never did go to Amoeba
but we kneeled at Puvunga

I cannot dream this highway vacant
nor assume these lights are godless

I always wonder where the ghosts are
& if they still celebrate the living

Headlights hush through our window
in the eternal language of the grasses

First Date

want my Luci Tapahonso cowboy
     with a shining belt
     and a good dog

he likes my legs in blue jeans
but even more,
       my poetry

we ride the moon's shirttails
     'til dawn
when we bless ourselves

and wade into the spring water,
       well-fed and wet faced

& while the sky turns to meteors
holographing

we're still drunk off Tennessee Honey

my mom's Revlon
sticking to the sugar

we break curses
       kissing in the corner booth
baby-blue bras
       hung from the ceiling
with George on the speakers

this is a place
      for a good gal like me

slicked in the grass
      by his leaning boots

under the warm shower
           of stars

Ancestors' wildest dreams

r drunk on the sticky floor
of a Denny's   texting gma Ayóó aníínishní
& crying in the same hot breath abt
not knowing the right word for apology

if one exists   keyboard smashing
resilience resilience reslienceResielance
as we delete IG so we don't
have to see ppl out-sacred-ing

each other. Maybe we're only sovereign
in bed   sometimes   drowning
in the dark & in the soft pools
of their eyes, living off the hard tack

of their thighs moving to an MCR mixtape
We froth   Ancestors' sleep paralysis
demon   caught in cold sweat & skipped
therapy   untangling our bodies

from sheets always untangling
hair out from under   somewhere
    fractals left in corners, under junip-
berry branches   Do we even remember

how gma baked her pies? The corn stalks
stretched higher than Holy People
that yr... & we came home buzzed
on lemonade   & an auntie's laughter...

Everyone is always talking about
    an ancestor that is or isn't
pleased
BUT—

I saw a strawberry moon tonight rising...
I learned the word in my language for laugh...
      We found it together:
Dloh   dloh dloh dloh
We eat it
We setting spray it to the page

Song for the black cat outside my mother's apartment

We know what it is to not be wanted,
when our bodies are taboo.

Night limbs, how our eyes
swallow everything

When I was brought into the world,
I looked back.

The trees were heavy with dark.
They say a wicked woman walks

bad luck. What makes a wicked woman?
Irises green with want, barbed tongues

to catch what's coming.
I want to move through the trees

as you do: four palms flush to the earth,
dark river with two wild torches

in a corner: living shadow, the same color
as forgetting.

How many lives
can I hold in each chamber

of my heart?

BLACKLIST ME

none of my ancestors are on the radio
none of my ancestors are
but my sister refurbished
an 8-track and I want ndn rock 'n' roll in her

purest form: NDNs huddled in a basement
somewhere, listening to bootlegged
tapes, except the basement's
not a basement. it's a truck bed—

(someone's uncle's GMC) wheedling
over a lip of river cuz
the best thing about rock 'n' roll is
you don't have to do anything right

to survive. you don't even have
to make sense to a white english
professor who wants chronology
when I want six strings and a truck careening

into the horizon. I want the explosion
as grand as cicadas amping
out the sound of night as the 8-track
rolls and rolls and my favorite singers

live forever instead of on
some balding president's blacklist,
and through the smoke I almost want
to mistake a splinter of moonlight

for Mildred Bailey's pinkie ring, all the NDNs
dusting themselves off
and laughing at the smolder,
the little wheel spin and spin
the little wheel spin

ACKNOWLEDGMENTS

"August" appears in the 2023 issues of *Poetry Northwest.*

"Ancestors' wildest dreams" is in the March 2023 issue of *Poetry.*

"Sound of under-water" is in the Winter issue of *The Adroit Journal.*

"Coming-of-age song" appeared in *The Worcester Review, 2023.*

"Your Return" is published in *Diode Poetry, 2022.*

"Navajo-English Dictionary" is published in *Cutthroat Journal,* 2023.

"Creation Story Blues" is published in *Poetry Online,* 2022.

"The year the An*sazi Inn burned down" appears in the March 2023 issue of *Poetry.*

"BLACKLIST ME" is published on Poets.org, 2022.

"You survive the end of the world in Kayenta, AZ with your mother" is published in *Third Coast Magazine,* 2023.

"Put on that KTNN" is published in *Black Warrior Review,* 2023.

"Wax Cylinder" is published in *Superstition Review,* Summer 2023.

"Alabama, 1992" appears in the Summer 2023 issue of *The Chapter House Journal (Institute of American Indian Arts).*

"Navajo Mountain" appears in *Peripheries Magazine, Fall 2023.*

"Notebook" and "Everything is stranger in the NE ..." appeared in *Sugar House Review in 2023.*